MW01292087

The Intimate GOD

Tricia Martin

Other Books by Tricia Martin

The Old Tree Series

The Old Tree

The Land of Bizia

The Kingdom of Knon

The Mild, Mild West

Into the Night Sky

Arabian Lights

One for All and All for One

Contents

The Intimate GOD

Tricia Martin

Chapter One

In the Beginning

In the beginning was the Word and the Word was with God and the Word was God. (John 1:1, New International Version)

When I was eight-years-old my family moved from California to London, England. An evangelist named Billy Graham was leading revival meetings in England at that time and my mother invited me, along with several girlfriends, to join her at one of his meetings that week.

I remember sitting up in the nosebleed section of an enormous stadium and listening intently to Billy Graham's inspiring message. I was awestruck by what he was saying and cried when he described this beautiful Jesus and what He had done in giving His life for me.

When the invitation was finally given to receive salvation during the altar call, I ran down row after row of stairs, my eyes brimming with tears, toward the foot of the platform where he stood waiting for those whose hearts had been moved to accept Jesus as their Savior.

Finally I arrived, with tears streaming down my young face. I gazed up at Billy Graham with amazement that such wonderful news was possible in a world where all I had experienced thus far was fear and trauma that had left my little heart bruised and broken. Up until that moment I was like a delicate china teacup that someone had smashed with a hammer and left shattered in pieces.

I gave my life to the Lord that day and everything began to change for the better from that point on. I embarked on a new journey that led me into more joy, a deeper sense of peace, and a new, wonderful relationship with a kind and loving God who cared deeply about me, even though I was a small and insignificant child.

My family finally moved back to California from England when I was 12. Sadly, my parents then separated after years of painful discord. I watched with deep sorrow as my father left our home to move permanently to New York City.

Despite the brokenness of our family, I continued to grow in my relationship with the Lord. I was 14 when my mother first told me about the baptism of the Holy Spirit. I asked her to show this to me in the scriptures and she did; especially pointing out the stories of those who had received the baptism of the Holy Spirit in the book of Acts.

I went into my room, closed the door, and proceeded to study intently the scriptures she had shown me. That night while lying in bed, I invited the Holy Spirit to come and baptize me and asked for the gift of tongues. The room filled with a comforting presence like warm oil, and a deep peace filled my body, mind, soul and spirit. I fell into a deep sleep that night embraced by the loving presence of God. I awoke the next morning with great joy as the gift of tongues poured from my mouth. The Father had heard my prayer!

From that point on I was able to talk to the Father and receive words back from Him in my mind. I wrote down each conversation between the Lord and me and still have that journal filled with those wonderful, intimate words.

Jesus promises in scripture that, *"My sheep hear My voice"* (John 10:27). I have found this to be true in my own life and believe that anyone who has accepted Jesus as their Savior and Lord has been given the same opportunity to hear His voice. Please don't think that He has to talk to you audibly (though some people have experienced this), but by faith **believe** what Jesus said and expect Him to communicate with you in many, many wonderful and unusual ways. *He is very creative*.

I have learned through the years that focusing our thoughts on Him helps to open up our hearts to hearing His voice.

As we sit in His presence, He fills

us with His love and gently uncovers areas of fear, unforgiveness, pain, sorrow, rejection, brokenness and self-centeredness. Then, as we open up these areas in our hearts and minds for healing, He floods us with His love and peace.

It is definitely a process but it works. I can testify to that. Everything we need is already within us, as the scripture declares:

The Kingdom of heaven is within you.
(Luke 17:21, King James Version)

Our job is to change our minds. That is, to alter the way we have been taught to think and feel, and **choose** with our **will** to believe that the Kingdom of Heaven and the Creator of all things lives within us. What a joy to know this!

My purpose in writing this book is to help you draw closer to the Father,

Son, and Holy Spirit; to receive more revelation of His deep and powerful love for you; to hear and know His voice, and to be filled with His Spirit. If a broken little child like me, whose life was filled with fear and trauma, can have a deep and loving relationship with Him, then everyone can be filled with His presence and peace.

Sometimes we have a difficult time hearing Him or feeling His presence. There are many reasons for this. One major reason can be attributed to the attitudes in our hearts, which I like to call *"issues of the heart."* These attitudes create noise within us which hinder or block our ability to hear His voice clearly and find rest in Him.

Let me define what I mean by issues of the heart. The scriptures say in Proverbs 4:23, *"Above all else, guard your heart, for everything you do flows from it."* When I speak about heart issues I am using the term loosely to describe our attitudes about life, the people around us (past as well as present), and the circumstances we face daily.

For more than twelve years now, I've taught a class at my church on the subject of intimacy with God and how to hear His voice. When I teach about heart issues, I bring three or four umbrellas to class and open them up one at a time; placing them all around me until I am surrounded and enclosed within a wall of umbrellas. The class can't see me as I begin to share the various heart issues that represent each umbrella. For example, I may say that my sister hurt my feelings and that I suppressed the pain until it festered and then turned into anger or offense. Then I talk to the Lord about that pain and come to the place of forgiving my sister and releasing her from my anger and offense. At that time I close the umbrella and move on to the next heart issue.

I may pick fear, bitterness,

ambition, jealousy, envy or rebellion against authority. The point is, when I address each heart issue with the Lord, an umbrella is closed and finally I am left standing with nothing blocking me from the Son-shine of His love and presence.

I then explain to my class that we need daily to seek His presence and sit with Him; examining our hearts to see if there is an umbrella open and blocking His love. This doesn't have to been a long drawn out process, just relational. Five minutes a day works to keep our relationship with Him open and unblocked.

In the later chapters I will address a few heart issues that Jesus spoke about in the Sermon on the Mount as examples of how we are to respond in our relationships with one another.

One of the heart issues we will

look at is fear. This can create noise between us and God, paralysis, and a general feeling of separation that prevents us from hearing His voice and feeling His presence. His love, and our choice to receive it at these times, will help eliminate the noise and emotional responses associated with fear.

Our Lord is all about relationship and He desires a close one with each of us. Just look at the Old Testament and God's love and passionate desire to have an intimate relationship with His people, Israel.

His Commandments are all about relationship and display His high regard for human life. We can position ourselves daily to hear His voice more clearly, much as John the beloved did at the last supper, as he leaned against the chest of Jesus.

Pay attention and take seriously what God shows you and says to you.

His still, small voice will speak to you in your thoughts more than you realize. Below is an example of how we can disregard His gentle voice inside our thoughts.

One day I was coming out of a store when I made the mistake of ignoring a quiet word of prompting. I got into my car and heard in my mind the words, "Don't back out to the left, back your car out to the right."

I looked behind me and saw a car waiting for my space to the right, blocking me. Because it was awkward to back out to the right, I disregarded the still small voice and turned my steering wheel to the left and proceeded to back out.

Suddenly, someone began to bang loudly on my rear window and as I looked back, I saw a man yelling at me. He ran to my driver's window and told me that a tiny, old woman had almost been hit by my car. She was too small for me to see in my rearview mirror as I turned around to look while backing out. Whew! The Lord helped me in that situation, but I never forgot the lesson He taught me.

That experience has helped me to value, even more, the quiet gentle voice in my thoughts and to pay attention even at the times His voice seems to be speaking very softly. Life is certainly easier when I do.

Above all else, guard your heart, for everything
you do flows from it.
(Proverbs 4:23)

Chapter Two

Intimacy

*I no longer call you servant…instead I have
called you friends. (John 15:15)*

I have discovered throughout
my life with the Lord that the most important and valuable part of my walk is
intimacy with Him. What do I mean by
intimacy? It is the act of being with the

Father, Jesus, and the Holy Spirit, in a place of rest and enjoyment of who they are and receiving their unconditional love into my heart.

Now I am not talking about sitting with the Lord in prayer to solve problems or deal with heart attitudes, although that does happen while being with Him.

No, I am talking about sitting with Him in a place of peace, maybe with music playing or outside in the backyard and welcoming His presence and then resting. It is the deliberate act of focusing on Him, or a scripture about Him, and by faith knowing that His presence is with me.

This can be a challenge at first because we are so accustomed to being busy from dawn 'til dusk; filling our lives with numerous activities. Or perhaps we are overwhelmed with personal problems or from pain that is shouting loudly within our hearts. At these times it becomes difficult to sit quietly with the Lord because of the endless thoughts and emotions that surface and produce the opposite of peace.

The practice of resting in the Lord is like a muscle; the more you use it the stronger it gets. I found it difficult at first to sit with the Lord because my mind wandered or painful memories surfaced. But over the years I have learned to open up those memories to Him and receive healing while in that special place of rest.

Sometimes trivial thoughts about my day would interrupt my time of rest. I had to practice gently pushing those thoughts aside and then re-focusing my attention back on Him - resting again in His loving arms while drinking in His peace. After growing up in such a fearful childhood, it was comforting to be flooded with inner peace and love.

It is necessary to learn to quiet our hearts and minds while resting in Him. It has been in these times that I have received some of the most powerful and important words of comfort, encouragement, and direction; despite the fact that I was not even seeking a word, but rather His precious presence.

Many do not recognize His voice because they are expecting Him to speak in a loud booming voice, or they want an angel to appear in front of them with a message. He can and does speak that way sometimes, however, most of the time the Lord speaks gently to us in our thoughts, or gives us a light, refreshing feeling or impression.

The key is to learn to distinguish His voice from our own thoughts. As we pay attention to what we think might be Him, we start to become familiar with the difference between our thoughts and His still, peaceful voice. As we, by faith, become more attentive to these gentle promptings, He will share more and more with us and instruct us in discerning the difference between His voice and our own thoughts.

Too often, we are dull to what we think He might be saying or telling us because we have not practiced paying attention to His still, small voice. We even forget the words, the love, and the impressions we had in His presence, as the world presses in around us.

What do we have to lose if we risk? By risk I mean actively pressing in to listen to the gentle promptings inside our minds. After all, it could actually be Him and joy of joys we could be hearing His voice! If the thoughts are not heavy or negative, but instead light, refreshing and peaceable, then it could be the Lord speaking. Remember, His sheep hear His voice. The scriptures do not say, *some* of His sheep hear His voice, or certain sheep hear His voice. No, it says that His sheep; anyone that loves and follows Him, hears His voice (John 10:27 KJV).

Our Father is loving and kind. Do you really think He would be angry with you for desiring to hear His voice and value what He might be saying to you? No! Rather, He delights in His children and wants to draw closer to us.

Many places in scripture describe how the Lord speaks to us in that *Still Small Voice*: Let's look at 1Kings 19:11:

And He said, Go forth, and stand upon the mount before the Lord. And, behold, the Lord passed by, and a great and strong wind rent the mountains and brake in pieces the rocks before the Lord, but the Lord was not in the wind; and after the wind an earthquake, but the Lord was not in the earthquake; and after the earthquake a fire, but the Lord was not in the fire; and after the fire a **still small voice.** *And when Elijah* *heard it, he wrapped his face in his mantle and went out and stood at the entrance to the cave.*

It is important to be able to distinguish between His voice and other manifestations. In the scripture above there was an earthquake, a great strong wind, and finally a fire. Sometimes the Lord comes violently, and at other times quite loudly. But most of the time we miss His presence because He comes as that **still, small voice**, while we are distracted and too busy to quiet ourselves and listen.

I want to share an experience that happened to me many years ago that reveals the power of God and His still, small, voice.

In 1992 I was living with my husband, Steve, in Coppell, Texas, with our four-year-old son. We decided to visit my family in Orange County, California, and while there, my sister and her boyfriend invited us to an Anaheim Vineyard renewal meeting. My husband offered to babysit our son so I could attend and I took him up on it.

When we arrived at the renewal meeting, so many people had shown up that we were redirected to an overflow room that was very crowded.

The renewal meeting in the main auditorium was being piped into our overflow room and we could hear the speaker inviting everyone to be filled afresh with the Holy Spirit. We all stood up and stacked our folding chairs against the back wall, standing with arms raised to be filled again. A woman in our room was holding a microphone and proceeded to give a very powerful prophecy. The Holy Spirit began to fall in the room as she spoke.

As the Spirit fell on me, I was thrown backward several feet into a stack of chairs; scattering them everywhere as I fell on top of the mess, completely "out" under the influence of the Holy Spirit. When I opened my eyes again, I was lying on the floor unable to move and the people and objects in the room had become very faint, hazy, and almost transparent.

Jesus walked up to me, but unlike the shadowy figures in the room, I could see Him very clearly. He knelt beside me and began to pray for me, while placing a white linen cloth over my body. He told me He was finishing the healing process as a result of the traumatic experiences I had endured in my childhood (at this time I had already received a great deal of inner healing and deliverance.)

Someone came up beside Jesus and knelt next to Him. He had the shape of a person but was like water, and fire…it is hard to describe. Jesus told me it was the Holy Spirit and together they ministered to me while I lay still.

Jesus knelt there beside me pouring His love into me for a long time, while ministering peace, joy, and healing. Because I was unable to move, I rested in His presence and simply received.

Two hours later I sat up and now could see the Anaheim Vineyard overflow room and the people in it clearly again. I stood up and my sister and her boyfriend kept asking me if I was alright. They thought I had hurt myself when I fell backward into the chairs and was out in the Holy Spirit for so long. I calmed their fears as they studied my face and I told them I felt nothing but deep peace.

I was never the same after that experience and, in fact, moved into a new season of peace and intimacy with the Lord unlike anything I had ever known. It was a glorious experience of deep healing and transformation within my heart, mind and emotions.

That remembrance demonstrates how God can work together with the Holy Spirit in a powerful way, yet with a gentle, quiet touch. Both were present with me during that life-changing experience. So, the Lord can knock us off our feet and send us flying, and He can also come with His tender peace and love that heals. It is all about relationship with Him and flowing with whatever He wants to do.

Above all else, guard your heart, for
everything you do flows from it.
(Proverbs 4:23)

Chapter Three

Hearing God's Voice

My sheep hear My Voice
(John 10:27)

In this book I am *not* going to address all of the ways the Lord communicates with us, because I want to focus on intimacy and our attitudes. The ability to hear, feel, see and know

Him is greatly affected by our attitudes and close relationship with Him.

In my class on hearing the voice of God, I enjoy showing my students the countless and creative ways that He communicates with us. If we truly believe the Creator of the universe is our friend and wants to spend time with us (which He does), then we will watch and listen for Him throughout our day. His peaceful, loving presence can keep us company day and night.

I attended college at San Diego State University and lived with a girlfriend in a downstairs apartment right next to the campus. One day I was reading my Bible and sipping on a cup of hot tea when I heard footsteps on the outside stairs leading to the upper apartment. I felt the Lord saying, "Get up and look out the peep hole of your door." So I ran to the door and peeked out. Springing down the stairs and scooting around the corner was a cute, young man going to get his mail.

As I stood at the door the Lord said, "He is the one you will marry." I thought, 'Oh thank you, Lord, he's cute!' Later that year, my roommate and I got to know this cute, young man and found out that his name was Steve and we became friends but he did not approach me to go out. Finally, after a year of waiting, I moved on to date other Christian men who were interested and I forgot about the word the Lord had given me.

We all graduated and two years later, I attended a reunion party down in San Diego, and low-and-behold, Steve was there as well. We started talking and from that day on we were inseparable. One year later, in 1978, we married. So you see, what the Lord told me came true even though I was 'she of little faith.'

In 2001 after being married many

years, my husband and I drove up to Newport Beach to rollerblade and bike ride. This was right after 9/11 and the airline industry was suffering to the point that several airlines were on the verge of closing down. For those of you who do not remember, a group of terrorist flew two planes full of passengers into the World Trade Center's twin towers in New York City, destroying the planes, buildings and passengers. Thousands were killed and injured in this attack and the airline industry took a nosedive as people canceled reservations right and left. Being an airline pilot himself, my husband Steve was very depressed, as he contemplated a future without a job. He had always dreamed of being a pilot and God had finally answered his prayer. He loved every minute that he flew.

As we sat outside a little hole in the wall restaurant in Newport Beach that day, gazing at the ocean, I noticed the sky was dark and overcast. My husband began sharing his heart with me and talked about his fears over the airline going out of business. During this same period of time his father was very ill as well, and Steve was sad about his dad's condition. We were the only ones able to care for Steve's father, which was both a heavy responsibility and expensive; adding to his need for an income.

As he continued to share his fears I felt an oppressive spirit descending and depression surrounding both of us. I looked up into the sky and noticed 60 crows circling right above our heads, screaming and screeching; the noise was deafening. Turning to Steve, I asked him to stop talking for a minute and look up. Feeling the Spirit of God, I pointed out that we were being attacked and needed to rebuke this and call upon the Lord.

Together we asked the Lord for help and Steve bound the fear and oppressive spirits surrounding us. We both told the Lord that we chose to trust Him in each situation we faced. Immediately, deep peace filled the atmosphere around us and replaced the fear and anxiety that had surrounded us. We now rested in the Lord's strong presence while the crows screeched overhead.

As we gazed at the ocean and the skyline for a few minutes in silence, we noticed, off in the distance, a large pure white bird flying slowly toward us. When it was over our heads, it encircled the large group of screeching crows above us and in unison they flew away. All that was left was the large snowy white bird circling above and a deep quiet and peace. Then, we watched as the bird flew away in the direction of the crows. At that moment a ray of cheerful sunshine broke out of the dark, menacing clouds. The oppressive feeling was gone and both of us felt the Lord's peace and confidence.

This is a beautiful example of how the Lord can speak to us if we are listening and watching. That day Steve and I could have permitted our circumstances to overwhelm us, but we instead called on our friend and God, and He came to our rescue.

Interestingly, nothing changed in our circumstances after that. Steve watched as his father became sicker and three months later, he died. Thankfully, two weeks before he passed away, Steve shared Jesus with him and we know he will be in heaven waiting for us. In addition, his company went through bankruptcy twice and the pilots were forced to forfeit all of their retirement to help the airline stay afloat. His pay was cut in half as well, but we thanked God that he still had a job, and we are still thankful.

My husband developed a closer walk with the Lord because of that experience. I share that story every year in my class because it builds up the student's faith and encourages them as they walk through the difficulties in their own lives.

The Lord is very relational and wants to walk closely with us. He doesn't always stop painful things from happening, but He walks through life's circumstances; helping us to view them differently as He comforts us. Everything is transformed by His wonderful, peaceful presence. He is truly my joy each day and I practice remembering that He is there with me, moment by moment.

So you see, God can speak to us through His creation, as in the example of the white bird. Another example of God speaking to us through His nature happened in 2005, during a time when several prophecies were circulating about many natural disasters coming to California. Hurricane Katrina had already devastated the Gulf coast and the Rita hurricanes had just hit the east coast, destroying everything in their path.

My son, age 15 at the time, suddenly jumped up from the dinner table and told me to follow him outside into the backyard. It was not raining at the time and had not rained for many days. But over our home and the homes all around us was the most vibrant, colorful rainbow I had ever seen.

As I gazed up with awe at its beauty, I felt God was speaking to me, saying that disasters will come and go, but that He also uses nature to bring joy, peace and safety. His safety is what I immediately felt as I looked at Genesis 9:12 (English Standard Version) "This is the sign of the covenant which I make between Me and you and every living creature that is with you...I set my bow in the cloud, and it shall be a sign of the covenant between Me and the earth."

I personally believe that God was letting me know that He is covering our region with His wings of protection, and I felt a deep joy and peace in that knowledge.

The Lord communicates with us in many different ways and not always by speaking to us. There are times He simply wishes us to rest with Him and drink in His presence in silence.

Above all else, guard your heart, for everything you do flows from it.
(Proverbs 4:23)

Chapter Four

Resting in Him

Be still and know that I am God
(Psalm 46:10, NIV)

As I have said several times before, there are many ways to experience the Lord and hear His voice. One of my favorites is resting and soaking to worship music until I find that place of peace in Him. Often in this place of rest, the Lord will speak to me;

however, I personally enjoy resting in Him not to receive anything, but just to *be* with Him.

Thoughts and scriptures from Him will flow into our minds when the soil of our hearts is filled with His peace. Inner peace is very important. We can face anything if we have deep peace inside our minds and hearts.

There are so many scriptures throughout the Bible about resting and soaking in His presence and peace. Below are my personal favorites:

Be still before the Lord and wait patiently for Him. (Psalm 37:7)

In repentance and rest is your salvation. In quietness and trust your strength. (Isaiah 30:15b)

Jesus often withdrew to lonely places and prayed. (Luke 5:16)

Go into your room and close the door

and pray to your Father, who is unseen. Then your Father, who sees what is done in secret, will reward you. (Matt 6:6)

One day I was studying Psalm 46:10: *"Be still and know that I am God."* and discovered that the word <u>still</u> in the Hebrew is *raphah* which means to abate, to cease, to stay, idle, and be still.

Then I found out the same word *raphah* means also to cure, to mend, to **heal**, to repair, to make whole.

So you see, resting in Him brings healing on the inside, as well as the outside. While we rest in His presence He reveals, then washes away sin, anxiety, fear; whatever it is we need at that time. Even when we fall asleep while soaking, His spirit continues to flood us with His peace and love.

There are two individuals that lived during the seventeenth century that I have enjoyed studying. One is a man named Brother Lawrence who served in a monastery as a cook. When reading his life story it is interesting to hear that prayer time was very difficult for him because he was unable to sit still for very long.

The other brothers would pray for hours, but because Brother Lawrence was not able to sit quietly for very long, he learned to focus on the Lord while he rattled around in the kitchen with his pots and pans. I love that imagery because I too, have spent many a day cooking, cleaning and doing laundry while focusing my thoughts on the Lord; practicing His presence. Housework takes on a whole new meaning in that frame of mind!

When Brother Lawrence found his mind wandering, he would simply bring his thoughts back to focus on Jesus again. He called this "practicing the presence of God," and became so disciplined at it, that people came from far and wide to sit with him and learn of his unusual intimacy with God. They remarked that they could feel God's presence tangibly when they were around him.

The other person I have been greatly impacted by is a woman named Madame Guyon. She came from a wealthy family but had great emotional pain in her early relationships; escaping to this wonderful place of peace and love with Jesus. Anywhere she was, she could close her eyes and picture the Lord and sit in His presence, sometimes for hours at a time, as she rested in His arms.

Brother Lawrence and Madame Guyon were very different in their approach to resting in the Lord, but both found the Lord's presence each and every day of their lives; Brother Lawrence while busy working and Madame Guyon by sitting still and quiet in her Beloved's arms.

Our God loves being in relationship with us so much that He doesn't have a rigid set of rules for drawing close to Him, but wants us to come freely and in our own unique way. Any heart full of love and passion will find a way to draw close to the heart of God.

During my classes I have the room quiet down and relax while playing Christian soaking music. You can try this at home. If you have difficulty with your mind wandering, then think of different scriptures like, "The Kingdom of God is within you." (Luke 17:21)

Try soaking for five minutes at first. Then try it again another day and soak a little longer. During the resting time you can also ask the Lord if He has something to say to you. If you sense He does, then write it down in a journal. I have journals scattered throughout many of the rooms in my home.

Why don't you find five minutes to soak this week? Put some worship music on; lie down on the floor with a pillow supporting your head. If you have back problems then put your feet up on the end of a bed or sofa with your knees bent. Now relax and listen to the words of the worship song, think of a scripture or just rest in Him. Invite the Holy Spirit to come and fill you up and then believe that He is there in you and around you.

Above all else, guard your heart, for everything
you do flows from it.
(Proverbs 4:23)

Chapter Five

Undercover

Have confidence in your leaders and submit to their authority, because they keep watch over you as those who must give an account. Do this so that their work will be a joy, not a burden, for that would be of no benefit to you. (Hebrews 13:17)

It is very important to value those in leadership over us. Their spiritual authority creates a covering in the realm of the Spirit against evil.

I have Pastor Mike, and my husband, Steve, as spiritual coverings over me; protecting me from the enemy.

The attitudes of our heart play a huge role in our protection. We can appear to be under the covering of our leaders, but actually be standing outside of that covering through offense, judgment, or rebellion. When that happens, then the enemy has grounds to attack and deceive us. (*Much like wolves look for stray or lone sheep that are not with their shepherd.*)

> *Let everyone be subject to the governing authorities, for there is no authority except that which God has established. The authorities that exist have been established by God.* (Romans 13:1)

This can be challenging for us to live out, especially if some of the leaders we have been under were abusive, or hurt us in some way. There are many people in authority we have come into contact with that may have left their mark: fathers, mothers, teachers, and pastors, just to name a few.

Watch your heart and your tongue. What you say will act as a mirror into the content of your heart!

You can, however, experience hurt from a leader without giving in to sin or rebellion. It's a matter of choosing to respond to the Spirit, not the flesh, in that situation. Trust the Lord. You can speak the truth to a leader, but guard your heart, because it is possible they may disagree with your viewpoint. By virtue of their authority, they make the final decision. In the book, A More excellent way[1], author Henry Wright explains that one roadblock to healing can be "Touching God's anointed ones through slander, gossip etc..."

Now, I am not implying that we have to renounce our faith in Jesus in order to obey an oppressive authority. Absolutely not!

---

[1] A More Excellent Way: A Teaching on the Spiritual Roots of Disease, by Henry W. Wright. Publisher, Whitaker House 2000

The story of David in 1 Samuel 18:9 is a wonderful example to us of how to submit to authority, even an authority that hates us and wants to kill us! David knew the importance of submitting to authority and God blessed him for it.

Let's look at the young man, David, who was told by a prophet that he would be the next king. Little did he know there would be a very long wait between that word and its fulfillment.

King Saul held the position that David had been promised by God. How easy it would have been to take matters into his own hands by removing Saul and placing himself as king.

But David understood God's ways and doing things by God's Spirit and timing. He waited for the Lord to remove Saul and then establish him as king. He chose the way of the Spirit, not the way of the flesh (or soul). He did it God's way and not his own way.

Look at Saul's attitude toward David: "...*from that time on Saul kept a jealous eye on David.*" And *"Saul told his son Jonathan and all the attendants to kill David."* (Samuel 19:1)

Now let's take a close look at David's heart attitude toward a leader who was not only jealous of him and treated him badly, but who actually wanted to kill him!

David crept up unnoticed and cut off a corner of Saul's robe. Afterward David was conscience-stricken for having cut off a corner of his robe. He said to his men, "The Lord forbid that I should do such a thing to my master, the Lord's anointed, or lay my hand on him; for he is the anointed of the Lord." (1 Samuel 24:4-6)

Sometimes we think our leaders are the ones responsible for us moving forward in ministry. But this is not true. It is God who decides when to elevate and promote us. The world views promotion differently than God does anyway. Being known and successful in the world's eyes is not the yardstick God uses.

Being known in heaven by our Father and Jesus is the true definition of success.

We can use concerns and issues with our leaders as an opportunity to examine past hurts with parents, teachers, spouses, bosses, or anyone in authority that has hurt or offended us.

Go to the Lord and ask Him to heal and wash you of past injuries. Many times our present problems are simply a reflection of unresolved issues with parents and other authority figures in the past.

Chapter Six

Faith and Love

I pray that you, being rooted and established in love, may have power, together with all the Lord's holy people, to grasp how wide and long and high and deep is the love of Christ and to know this love that surpasses knowledge. (Ephesians 3:17b-19a)

I have struggled with fear throughout my entire life, yet the Lord has done much healing in me over the years. He floods my heart and mind with His love and peace daily and transforms my brokenness into strength and wholeness. And He whispers in my ear, "You are so safe," as he holds me in his arms.

His love is the most powerful force on our planet. I believe the Church tends to think of God's love as sweet and nice, which it is, but they often dismiss it in the area of His power. By that I mean His power is actually seen in His love. This love is a vital weapon to wield against the enemy's kingdom, which is based on fear and lies. How powerful God's love is in completely defeating those fears and lies.

I did have good experiences in my childhood; it wasn't all painful. For one thing, I knew my mother and father loved me because they told me and showed me. However, as with so many of us, along with the good there was also trauma, brokenness and pain. The Lord is so good to provide a way for us to be healed and move into a loving relationship with Him and one another.

In Chapter One I mentioned attending a Billy Graham Crusade in England when I was a child. We had moved to the UK when I was eight and the worse time for my entire family began, filled with fear and depressing events. My parent's marriage ultimately failed and during that same season I had several new traumatic experiences that added further injury to my heart, mind, soul and spirit. There even was an incident late one night in which a homeless man broke into our home. Although I was not harmed, this added again to my deep sense of vulnerability and unsafety. But the Lord is a redeeming God and never leaves or forsakes us.

As a result of these traumatic events, I was overwhelmed with fear. I would read my Bible and search out the scriptures about being safe but I struggled to believe this. The fear overpowered me at times, but I slowly, step-by-step, began to believe the truth about his love and protection.

Gradually, over many years, I did feel His love, but didn't happen all at once. When I look back I realize how much He has healed the inner places within me. Faith comes by hearing the Word of God.

My husband and I returned to England recently. We visited the very home that I had experienced all the trauma. But it had somehow changed, just as I had changed. A new family lived there now and this time I felt nothing but peace and the Lord's presence in and around me.

Through the years the Lord has reinforced His love for me through my husband, my mother, my family, friends, my church and soaking alone with Him.

There are several scriptures I would like to show you, but before I do, let's look at the definition of love in the **Strong's Concordance**:

Love- *To have delight in, to have affection for, to cling to, to be compassionate toward and to be merciful to.*

Now let's look up the word Fear.

Fear- *Fright, terror, dread, alarm, timidity, and faithlessness.*

There are so many scriptures on love in the Bible; it is full of them. Below are a few of my favorites. The first one is my life scripture because His love has truly changed me from the inside out.

I pray that you, being rooted and established in love, may have the power, together with all the Lord's holy people, to grasp how wide and long and high and deep is the love of Christ, and to know this love that surpasses knowledge—that you may be filled to the measure of all the fullness of God. (Ephesians 3:17b-19a)

Let Him kiss me with the kisses of His mouth, for your love is more delightful than wine. (Song of Songs 1:2)

My Beloved spoke and said to me, "Arise my darling, my beautiful one, and come with me. See! The winter is past: the rains are over and gone. Flowers appear on the earth; the season of singing is come, the cooing of doves is heard in our land... Arise, come, my darling; my beautiful one, come with me." (Song of Sg 2:10-13)

There are just as many scriptures on not being afraid.

Do not be afraid, Abram. I am your shield, your very great reward. (Genesis 15:1b)

Be strong and courageous. Be strong

and courageous. Do not be afraid; do not be discouraged, for the Lord your God will be with you wherever you go. (Joshua 1:6)

Do not fear, for I have redeemed you; I have summoned you by name; you are mine. When you pass through the waters I will be with you; and when you pass through the rivers, they will not sweep over you. When you walk through the fire you will not be burned; the flames will not set you ablaze. For I am the Lord you God, the Holy One of Israel, your savior. (Isaiah 43:1b-3a)

For God has not given us the spirit of fear; but of power, and of love and of a sound mind. (2 Tim 1:7, KJV)

I want to look more closely at one scripture that highlights fear and how Jesus responded to it in His disciples. The disciples were in a simple fishing boat traveling across the Sea of Galilee with Jesus in the stern, fast asleep.

Mark 4:35 -*That day when evening came, Jesus said to His disciples, "let us go over to the other side." Leaving the crowd behind, they took Him along, just as He was, in the boat... A furious squall came up, and the waves broke over the boat, so that it was nearly swamped. Jesus was in the stern, sleeping on a cushion. The disciples woke Him and said to him, "Teacher, don't you care if we drown?" He got up, rebuked the wind and said to the waves, "Quiet! Be Still!" Then the wind died down and it was completely calm. He said to His disciples. "Why are you so afraid? Do you still have no faith?" They were terrified and asked each other, "Who is this? Even the wind and the waves obey him?"*

One thing we need to be aware of with this story in Mark is that the danger was very real. The Sea of Galilee is surrounded by mountains. It is the largest freshwater lake in Israel and well below sea level (close to 700 feet), making it the lowest freshwater lake on earth. Cool air from the Mediterranean funnels down through the mountains to clash with the hot, humid air on the lake causing sudden violent storms. The danger was real for the disciples in that simple, little fishing boat as the waves splashed over the sides filling it with water. In fact, in Luke 8:23 it says they were in "great danger."

Nevertheless, each time I have read this story I always wonder why the disciples were so frightened. After all, it is clear that these seasoned fishermen of Galilee were not weak or timid by nature and had seen Jesus perform many miracles. But to their credit, they were facing a true emergency and their lives were in jeopardy. So you would think that when they woke Jesus up, He would have comforted them after calming the storm. But instead, He responded with, *'Why are you so afraid? Do you still have no faith?"*

I remember one time when my husband and I had taken some friends out to Lake Mojave. We were in a small ski boat and the weather started getting rough and the tiny ship was tossed (remember Gilligan's Island). I became frightened and a little tense so I can relate to the disciples in this situation. Their boat was in the center of a violent storm and filling up fast with water.

How many times have we felt that Jesus was fast asleep in our boat while all around us frightening things were happening?

This event is described in three of the gospels: Matthew, Mark and Luke. In all three accounts, Jesus asks the disciples why they are so afraid and where is their faith. Remember they had been watching Him perform miracles, feed thousands of people, heal leprosy and even raise people from the dead. But they still did not understand.

Even while writing this book, I have talked to the Lord about my fearful heart. After more than 50 years of walking with Him, how similar I am to these disciples. There are still areas of fear in my heart but the Lord challenges me with His words, "Do you have no faith?"

I looked up the definition of the word *faith* in Hebrews 11:1: "Now faith is confidence in what we hope for and assurance about what we do not see."

The Apostle Paul, the writer of the book of Hebrews, goes on to talk about Cain and Abel. The reason Abel's sacrifice was accepted by God was that he offered it by faith. Cain had the wrong heart attitude and gave his offering out of habit and obligation, whereas Abel gave the best and most generous portion he could give. We know this because Paul points out that by faith Abel offered God a better sacrifice than Cain. This implies that Cain's sacrifice was offered without faith and "without faith it is impossible to please God, because anyone who comes to him must believe that he exists and rewards those who earnestly seek him." (Hebrews 11:6)

So the heart issue the disciples faced in that little boat on the Sea of Galilee was not the violent storm, but rather their *lack of faith* in Jesus. I, too, need more faith to dispel my fears, but how do I do this? Jesus says, "Ask and it will be given to you, seek and you will find, knock and the door will be open to you." (Matthew 7:7). All I have to do is ask Him for the faith and then believe that I have now received it.

Fear, and lack of faith seem to be recurring themes that Jesus confronted most with His disciples. Even Joshua was being told over and over again, "Be strong and courageous". You don't keep saying that to someone who has enough faith.

While Jesus slept in the boat, I wonder if He was waiting for the disciples to use the authority He had given and shown them in the miracles He performed. What if one of the disciples had commanded the storm to stop in the name of Jesus? We will never know, but one definition for fear is faithlessness.

We need to remember and meditate on those times in our past when the Lord helped us in scary situations or impossible circumstances. He always came through with healing, comfort, provision.

How do you get out of a place of fear? One way is through soaking and resting in the Lord. Another way is to read scriptures about His deep love for you and invite the Holy Spirit to come and bring His healing presence in the places of fear. Rebuking fear, insecurity, and lies from the enemy, in the powerful name of Jesus also helps. Of course, going to church, worshipping and receiving prayer from family and friends, even a counselor, can be very beneficial as well.

Right now, pray and ask Jesus for an impartation of His love to flood and wash over any place in your mind, heart, or memories where there might be lingering fear. Trust me, He will come and heal those places.

Above all else, guard your heart, for everything you do flows from it.
(Proverbs 4:23)

Chapter Seven

Love

If I speak with the tongues of men and of angels, but do not have love I am a resounding gong or a clanging cymbal. If I have the gift of prophecy and can fathom all mysteries and all knowledge and if I have a faith that can move mountains but do not have love, I gain nothing. (1 Corinthians 13:1-3)

In my class on intimacy and heart issues, I focus on the topic of love more than anything else. That is why I have placed another chapter in this book on this subject. God has more to say about LOVE.

I Corinthians 13 is called the *Love Chapter* and warns that if I speak with the tongues of men and angels, and if I prophecy, command mountains to be thrown into the sea, and give up my body as a martyr, but don't love, it profits me nothing.

When the Apostle Paul wrote this chapter and spoke of giving his body to be burned, he was talking about someone giving his life for the Christian cause. "Surrendering my body to the flames" is a reference to becoming a martyr. It seems that even the supreme sacrifice of laying down one's life gains nothing for God's glory, without the right heart attitude.

All of the ministry and works we do for God amount to nothing if we do not have His love flowing from us. This section of scripture even says we sound like a *"loud, clanging cymbal"* when we minister without love.

LOVE IS:

Patient and Kind
Not envious
Not boastful
Not proud
Not rude
Not self-seeking
Not easily angered
Keeps no record of wrongs
Finds no joy in evil
Always protects
Always trusts
Always hopes
Always perseveres
LOVE NEVER FAILS

We cannot drum these attributes up in our own strength; these are the Fruits of the Spirit, formed deep in our hearts. The Holy Spirit, through the process of sanctification, changes our hearts through life's experiences.

The gifts cease to be powerful and glorify God when we use them without love.

Sometimes He tells me to give a very simple word about His love to someone and they start to cry, or are visibly touched. It's not about quantity, but quality. It's not about ministry, but relationship. It's not about self, but others.

Right now, ask the Lord to show you people in your church, in your family, and at work that you don't like or love. Ask Him to show you how He sees them and to give you His love for them as well.

We can receive His love by faith, simply by sitting and inviting Him to fill us. Love will flood our hearts when we spend time alone with Him and practice His presence. It also comes from understanding the intimacy and love Jesus and His Dad have given us.

If we allow Him to overflow our hearts with love, then our motive will be to love others through whatever gift we use. Did you know that our heart motive is huge to God? The Lord does not want us striving and performing, but operating from a position of sitting in Father God's lap and in Jesus' arms. How can you not love when you minister from that place of safety and peace?

1 Corinthians 1:2 states, *"To the church of God in Corinth, to those sanctified in Christ Jesus and called to be His holy people, together with all those everywhere who call on the name of our Lord Jesus Christ--their Lord and ours."* The word "sanctified" means to make holy, precious, set apart for the Lord, in our emotions, mind, will and thoughts.

We have both our old nature and our new nature, or spirit-man, co-existing within us always striving with each other. Therefore, we must make a choice daily to serve the Holy Spirit and do things His way. It's a matter of choice.

It is the same with our giftings, ministry, or whatever we are doing for God. If we do not release control to the Spirit, then we will be operating in our flesh and building our own kingdoms, not His; building ourselves up instead of glorifying Him.

In the New Testament, the scriptures often refer to His church as the Bride. In the Lord's eyes His bride is pure and spotless because of what Jesus accomplished on the Cross. The scriptures teach that the Kingdom of Heaven is within us. We have all we need from Him already available within us. However, there is still the ongoing process of choosing daily to become more like Him and crucifying the ways of our old nature. Beloved, I know you want to partner with Jesus in building His Father's Kingdom.

Love is a powerful weapon. It is not passive, but very active. Love is the most important of all foundational truths. If love toward God and people is the motive behind our ministry, then He will flow out of us in both the fruit and the gifts of the Spirit to bless many.

Here are a few more scriptures on love:

Perfect Love drives out fear. (1 John 4:18b)

As the Father has loved Me, so have I loved you. Now remain in My love...My commandment is this: Love one another as I have loved you. (John 15:9, 12)

The Lord your God is with you, the Mighty Warrior who saves. He will take great delight in you: in His love He will no longer rebuke you, but will rejoice over you with singing. (Zephaniah 3:17)

In Mark 12:30 Jesus gives the greatest commandment of all. "*Love the Lord your God with all your heart and with all your soul and with all your mind and with all your strength...love your neighbor as yourself. There is no commandment greater than these."* This was already given in the Old Testament as well, *"Love the Lord your God with all your heart, with all your soul and with all your strength." (Deuteronomy 5:6)*

Right now, invite God to fill you with a deeper, more passionate love for Him.

Above all else, guard your heart, for everything
you do flows from it.
(Proverbs 4:23)

Chapter Eight

Preferring One Another

Each of you should look not only to your own
interests but also to the interests of others.
(Philippians 2:3b-4)

In Philippians it says: *"Therefore
if you have any encouragement from being
united with Christ, if any comfort from his
love...then make my joy complete by being
like-minded, having the same love, being one
in spirit and purpose. Do nothing out of*

selfish ambition or vain conceit. Rather, in humility value others above yourselves, not looking to your own interests but each of you to the interests of others. In your relationship with one another, have the same mindset as Christ Jesus: Who, being in very nature God, did not consider equality with God something to be used to His own advantage, rather, he made himself nothing by taking the very nature of a servant" (Phil. 2:1b-7)

Wow! There certainly is meat in these verses and a blueprint for relating to one another! In a world of relational chaos and brokenness these scriptures are an arrow shooting straight to the heart of God. If we ever needed counsel and wisdom on how to relate to one another inside the church and out, well, here it is.

How do we live these truths out? The key lies in allowing the Lord to transform our heart attitudes by forming the fruit of His Spirit within us.

This can be a very painful process, but there is no other way to do it, we have to die to ourselves. The death to self is not about the true self, but rather, the old way of thinking, feeling and reacting. We have the nature of God within us so it is simply a matter of choice. As we choose God the old self will diminish and the fruit of His Spirit will grow stronger within us.

Many, many years ago I was leading a prayer group and I was insecure about its small attendance. By this time I had worked through several heart attitudes and issues to do with envy and comparing myself with others. I thought I no longer had jealousy or envy toward anyone, and so I assumed most of my heart issues were healed in this area. Then a friend started a group on the exact day and time as mine. Her group drew a larger crowd and I began to compare her group to mine. Anytime you do this you will begin to feel insecure and uneasy.

A short time later I was resting with the Lord and He gently told me to look at my feelings about this situation. I told Him that I wasn't jealous because He had already healed me of that. He was so gentle and kind when He responded that actually what I was feeling was *jealousy* but it was subtle. I sighed at the time, realizing He was right and asked Him to forgive me. Right at that moment He poured His safety and love into me and reminded me that He was my source of security and that He would take care of my life, ministry, everything.

I changed my attitude immediately and actually began to refer people to my friends' group; praying blessings on it. Well, you guessed it, my group began to grow and prosper as well! Because I had allowed Jesus to secure me in His love, it really didn't matter anymore what happened to either group as *that* was no longer my focus, *He* was. Funny how the Lord will orchestrate situations to show us what lies hidden in our hearts and then help direct us into the right attitude.

I have heard the word "envy" defined as wanting what someone else has and the feeling that they have an advantage over us. Likewise, "jealousy" has been defined as wanting to protect our position when we perceive that someone else is moving up a little too fast and might threaten to take it from us. Can you see how this could be lethal in the church community? The Pharisees felt jealousy toward Jesus and were very threatened by Him. When we feel jealousy or envy, this becomes an opportunity to invite the Lord to wash and purify these heart attitudes

We will continue to have these feelings as long as we keep comparing ourselves with others around us and feel we are inadequate or fall short. These feelings originate from our brokenness and self-worth issues. But the cure is to get our eyes off ourselves and on to the Lord:

The Lord wants us to build up and encourage one another in our churches and in our lives in general. Our relationships, the workplace and our ministries are no place to strive for position or promotion, but rather, to help others find their place so they can become the most effective in glorifying Jesus. We don't have to worry about being overlooked as it is the Lord who positions us, opens doors, and uses our giftings in His perfect way.

We need to have a humble attitude. The world's system promotes competition and striving. The Kingdom of God fills us with peace, simplicity and humility, so we can choose the Kingdom's way when we are in an intimate relationship with Jesus and our Father. Spending time alone with the Lord and soaking helps solve our heart issues. As we rest in His presence everything else pales in comparison and our identity gets re-focused back into Him. Then, when someone is promoted or receives what we wanted, we can praise God as He is glorified through them. In football, team members rally to help block for the player who has the ball because they all want him to make a touchdown. We want the person in the limelight to make a touchdown for Jesus.

When I was 12- years-old my family moved back to the United States from England. My father took us to our new home, which was huge and beautiful. My older sister received a lovely room with a balcony overlooking the rose garden and she and my older brother had their very own bathrooms as well. My three younger brothers had a large room three times the size of a normal one to share between them.

I waited in anticipation for my room, but it never came. It appeared that they had forgotten me and there were no more rooms! I immediately felt all the familiar feelings of being overlooked, discounted, rejected, not valued or important. Finally, my mom had an idea to convert a small room that had once served as a powder room with a tiny bathroom, into a bedroom for me. She painstakingly transformed it into a precious room just for me.

The room was halfway up the stairs, which made me feel half as valuable as everyone else, as I gazed up the stairs at the rest of my family. It is when we contrast what we have to what others have, that we can feel small and insignificant. Had it been any other situation and I was given that room, I would have been ecstatic. But these circumstances made me feel invisible and less than my other brothers and sister.

I have received tremendous healing from the Lord over the issue of feeling valuable, among other issues. As with many of us, my injuries were repeated over and over again, but Jesus has stepped in, each time, like a Master Healer, giving me a choice to forgive and come to him to receive healing, safety and value.

Recently the Lord took me back to those memories of that little room halfway up the stairs and told me it had been a gift from him all along. He said, "Change the way you look at this." As he said this I saw a vision of him sitting in that little room on my bed, but this time He was surrounded by deep, rich, velvet. I looked around to see the walls embedded with jewels; the furnishings looking like they were from a palace with vats of warm oil in several places around the room. He told me He had blessed me with my own room because it was there that He had filled me with His Spirit and began a journey of deep intimacy with me. I realize now that God allowed that situation to make me who I am today. My deep need for him was only accentuated by that experience when I was 12.

Although very painful, it really doesn't matter where we find ourselves because if He is there with us, then the trauma and pain we experience becomes a place of transformation and beauty when he moves into it. (Note: I found out many, many years later when I was an adult that my parents miscounted the rooms and thought there was another room next to my sister's.)

When we feel unloved, over-looked, unnoticed, discounted and have other injuries from parents or authority figures, this can leave deep wounds and gaping holes in our hearts. We start to compare ourselves with those around us and to feel envy, jealousy, bitterness and self-pity, then, that emotional noise creeps in between us and our Beloved, making it harder to hear His voice clearly. We must let Him heal the pain that caused these injuries so that our hearts can rest again in Him and listen to His words of love and comfort.

Jesus come into these wounds and heal them with your love!

Chapter Nine

Godly versus worldly ambition

Do nothing out of selfish ambition or vain conceit. Rather, in humility value others above yourselves. (James 2:3)

The Lord has placed a longing to be successful and "great" into the hearts of all His children. While this can be an honorable endeavor, it can also become a serious problem when we try to fill that longing in the wrong ways out in the world and in the church.

In his book, <u>The Seven Longings of the Human Heart</u>,[2] Mike Bickle states:

"God has given us the gift of greatness that lasts forever. It has nothing to do with how big our ministries are, how big our bank accounts, are how many people like us, or how many people get healed when we pray for them. It is something that transcends all of these realities."

Our value and greatness is already settled in the eyes of God!

In this world system we are taught to manipulate others, achieve more, and push and shove to achieve our goals and position on the stage of life. The <u>Webster's Dictionary</u> defines ambition as: an ardent desire for rank, fame or power. Quite obviously, the focus is on self.

---

[2] <u>Seven Longings of the Human Heart</u>, by Mike Bickle with Deborah Hiebert. Publisher, Charisma House – A Strang Company 2006

But in the Lord's kingdom we must focus on Jesus, His father and the Holy Spirit; not self. When we focus on those around us and build them up, we are demonstrating the opposite spirit of ambition. Relationship with the Lord, family, and friends needs to be our primary focus. Too many people become obsessed with their gifting or ministry and forget the most important thing; *relationship*. The purpose of the gifts and ministry is to glorify the Lord and build up his people.

When we study Philippians 2:7-9 we are given the example of Jesus *"who humbled himself by becoming obedient to death, even death on a cross. Therefore God exalted Him to the highest place and gave Him the name that is above all names."* So, there is an ambition that builds our own kingdom, and there is an ambition that builds God's Kingdom. I believe that worldly ambition is about self and is rooted in a broken identity that we are trying to heal. But Godly ambition is a passionate desire for the Lord to further His kingdom here on this planet.

It is essential that we become very secure in our relationship with Jesus, the Father, and the Holy Spirit. They are more than enough for us. Our work for the Lord can then come from a place of intimacy and rest in Them.

Above all else, guard your heart, for everything
you do flows from it.
(Proverbs 4:23)

Chapter Ten

The Bridegroom

For the wedding of the Lamb has come and His
bride has made herself ready.
(Revelation 19:7)

*As a bridegroom rejoices over his
bride, so will your God rejoices over
you.* (Isaiah 62:5)

*Let us rejoice and be glad and give
Him glory. For the wedding of the
Lamb has come and His bride has
made herself ready. Fine linen, bright
and clean was given her to wear.*
(Revelation 19:7-8)

I will betroth you to me forever; I will betroth you in righteousness and justice, in love and compassion. I will betroth you in faithfulness and you will acknowledge the Lord. (Hosea 2:19-20)

Jesus is our bridegroom and our friend. The bridal relationship is the most intimate of all relationships. If God tried to pick an earthly relationship to portray intimacy, He could not have pick anything deeper and more personal than that of the bride and the bridegroom. Everything is fresh, pure, new and beautiful when a man and woman are first married. So with Jesus, His love for us is always fresh and pure - filled with passion.

Did you ever wonder what Jesus meant in John 14:20?

On that day you will realize that I am in My Father and you are in Me, and I am in you.

He was sharing with His disciples the wonderful revelation that after He died on the cross and was raised from the dead, they would be filled with the Holy Spirit and He and His Father would live within them. The Kingdom of Heaven would be within them! Everything they needed would be right inside their hearts, minds, souls and spirits. The key would be to believe, by faith, that this was true and to allow the Holy Spirit to put the old nature to death daily. The choice would be theirs to turn to the Lord, who now lived inside them, for help in crucifying the old ways of thinking, feeling and believing.

Jesus said as He and His Father are One so He wants to be one with us. This revelation is spiritually discerned and spiritual in nature. The human marriage is an echo of the relationship between Jesus and His Church.

The Spirit will lead us to go with

Him out into the highways and byways to share the love of God with those in the world. This is good; very good. But we need to fiercely protect our precious time alone with Him, as we sit in His presence. This state of "being" is more difficult than "doing", especially in our culture. He delights in us and enjoys the times we join Him in that state of being together and resting.

We desperately need to know this deep love that He feels for us. It has no strings attached and He loves us intrinsically (belonging to the essential nature). We can rest in Him with no *requirements* to do anything but simply be with Him. Because He fills us with His love, we then desire to go out with Him and further His Kingdom down on this planet; bringing glory back to our Beloved. The motive is not from striving or working for His approval but from a place of rest and intimacy with Him.

In the Gospel of Luke, Jesus

talked about two sisters named Mary and Martha. He said that Mary had chosen the better portion and it would not be taken away from her. Luke 10:40 recounts the story:

> As Jesus and His disciples were on their way, He came to a village where a woman named Martha opened her home to Him. She had a sister called Mary, who sat at the Lord's feet listening to what He said. But Martha was distracted by all the preparations that had to be made. She came to Him and asked, "Lord, don't you care that my sister has left me to do the work by myself? Tell her to help me!" "Martha, Martha," the Lord answered, "you are worried and upset about many things, but only one thing is needed. Mary has chosen what is better and it will not be taken away from her." (Luke 10:38-42)

For centuries, Martha, has been

misunderstood as people try to interpret the words of Jesus. She was, in fact, doing a wonderful and precious act of service by cooking and feeding those around her. However, when it took away from her intimacy with Jesus, well, that was the key to His statement. She was upset with Mary for sitting at the Lord's feet and listening to Him, rather than helping her.

As Jesus looked into Martha's heart, He told her that Mary had chosen the better portion and it would not be taken away. The key here is the heart. Mary was sitting at His feet while He taught, Martha was in another room distracted. I wonder if Jesus wanted Martha to give Him one hundred percent of her attention for a little while and then when He moved out to minister, she would as well. Jesus said He only did what His Father was doing, and possibly Martha was busy with good works, but not aware of what Jesus and His Father were doing.

When Mary sat at the feet of Jesus, I believe this was about intimacy; not about works. Mary had found her Beloved One and was not going to be distracted, as she sat at the His feet and listened intently to Him. Jesus noticed this enough to comment about her to His disciples.

I was at the International House of Prayer (IHOP) in Kansas City, Missouri, many years ago, at one of their prophetic conferences on Bridal Intimacy. During the worship I closed my eyes and saw Jesus dressed in a white tuxedo coming up to me with His arms outstretched to dance. He looked just like a bridegroom as He took me in His arms and began to dance with me. As I gazed into His face I was overwhelmed by the deep love, peace, kindness, gentleness and passion being communicated through His eyes. I felt loved down to the core of my being.

This is how Jesus and our Father

always feel toward us. We can sit, rest and soak with Them at any time; allowing Them to wash away our distractions and offenses, anger, feelings of loneliness, depression, sorrow, insecurity…the list goes on and on. While soaking, we re-align with Jesus and His Father and the Spirit. Things that worry or hurt us can be immediately dealt with and washed away in His tender love, kindness and care. It reminds me of having a chiropractic adjustment.

Right now, rest in the Lord's arms and allow Him to fill you up. Give Him your burdens and receive His peace and love. Remember, the Kingdom of Heaven is within you.

Chapter Eleven

Dreams

For God does speak - now one way, now another - In a dream, in a vision of night, when deep sleep falls on men and they slumber in their beds. (Job 33:14-15)

I wanted to add this subject to my book because the Lord has given me dreams that have been instrumental in changing the direction of my life.

As a young woman, just after high school graduation, I headed down to San Diego State University and eventually received a Bachelor's degree in Psychology and went on to receive my Master of Arts in Counseling.

During my first year at SDSU, I joined a sorority at my mother's suggestion. It was a way to get to know people in a school of 30,000 students. I was a born again spirit-filled Christian, but I was also somewhat confused at the time, as you will see in my story. My sorority sisters and I went to many parties where there was drinking, a few drugs and wild behavior.

I personally stayed away from the drugs and wild behavior; however, I joined them in drinking and having fun. They voted me the chaplain of the sorority because I would share about Jesus at their parties, while I was drinking (I know it doesn't make sense, but I was confused). Anyway, after several months of this lifestyle I had a dream that left me with great concern.

When I awoke I was shaken and knew this was a prophetic dream and I was being warned about something. I had been walking with the Lord for eight years by that time and had the scriptures deep inside my heart. My mother had also been a valuable mentor for me, and so I immediately called her.

She told me the dream was a serious warning about my walk with the Lord and the lifestyle I was living. She said I had a decision to make and that the enemy was influencing me. That week I went straight to my sorority and told them all that I would be dropping out of the sorority permanently. I went on to say that I was a Christian and was not able to join them in their partying anymore.

I sent a letter of resignation to the national board of the sorority and received a rude and angry response back. They stated that they were, in fact, a Christian sorority and how dare I suggest otherwise. Well, after that experience I re-dedicated my life fully to the Lord and spent the next year alone, sitting on the grassy hills of SDSU playing my acoustic guitar and worshipping the Lord. It was a solitary time, but I grew very close to Him during that season.

I ended up meeting a group of 15 wonderful Christian students. We all had such fun together and I eventually met my husband through this group.

So you see, we need to pay attention to our dreams, they can change the course of our life.

Most dreams are not warnings but I believe any dream we remember can reveal to us what we are processing at the time. Some dreams will be prophetic invitations from the Lord to move us into something new. This is just one more creative way that He speaks to us.

I have noticed with dreams that it is easy to become distracted by all the details. I generally ask the Holy Spirit to highlight the central theme and five to seven elements that I am to focus on in that dream. I also don't have a rigid rule guide for interpretation, but know the Lord is all about relationship, so I ask Him how to precede with each dream. Sometimes He has me call a friend or share it with my husband to get their input. He may ask me to look a word up in the Strong's Concordance, which is a wonderful tool that takes individual words from the scriptures and provides a definition of them in the original Greek and Hebrew text. He has also had me look up something from my dream in an ordinary dictionary and then, by the Spirit, highlights a definition that He wants me to apply to the dream.

I recently learned additional information about interpreting dreams from an international prophetic leader who was very gifted in the area of interpreting dreams through a biblical model. I have incorporated much of his valuable information into all that the Lord has shown me through the years.

The key is to be open and spontaneous with God about your dreams. Read the books on interpreting dreams; but then be ready for the Lord to prompt you to interpret your dream in a quite different way. *"Do not interpretations belongs to the Lord" (Genesis 40:8)* stated Joseph so long ago when he spoke to Pharaoh. The truth still applies today. There were no books back then on how to interpret dreams but he had the Lord and that was enough.

Above all else, guard your heart, for everything you do flows from it.
(Proverbs 4:23)

Chapter Twelve

Go Fly Your Kite

I have come that you may have life and have
it to the full (John 10:10)

In wrapping up all the principles
I have offered in this book, I believe it's
important to mention that forgiveness is
a central issue in following Jesus and

becoming more like Him. Throughout life we experience many traumas, rejections, injuries and wounds. It is vital that we practice forgiveness in order to be healthy and foster wholeness in all our relationships, even with the Lord Himself.

> *You have heard that it was said, 'love your neighbor and hate your enemy.' But I tell you, love your enemies and pray for those who persecute you, that you may be children of your Father in heaven. He causes His sun to rise on the evil and the good, and sends rain on the righteous and the unrighteous. If you love those who love you, what reward will you get?* (Matthew 5:43-46)

We must learn to accept our imperfections and those in others, knowing that Jesus died on the cross for us all. This helps us to treat ourselves and our relationships with others in a spirit of humility and kindness.

Listening is the highest honor we can extend to another person. Truly listening, without waiting to jump in and give our opinion is difficult, but we can learn to do this. It is especially difficult to listen when we have been hurt or offended by the other person, but also very important. Ask the Holy Spirit to transform this area of your life.

I grew up in a family where all eight members were constantly talking at once, so this has been an especially difficult area for me. But Jesus has not given up on changing my heart, habits, and listening skills. In the years that have come and gone, I have learned to forgive and release those who deeply wounded and injured me when I was a young girl. Now I pray for them and feel love toward them because of the forgiveness I've extended. I have been set free from the prison of their terrible choices through the act of forgiveness.

When we trust the Lord in every

situation, no matter how painful, He forms a deep peace inside us that nothing can shake. No matter what happens to us, we know that He is good and loving, and will eventually work everything together for our good.

When Jesus hung on that cruel cross 2,000 years ago He said, *"Father forgive them for they do not know what they are doing" (Luke 23:34).* We must echo that heart cry when we are abused, battered, cruelly treated and shamed. He will set us free to love and bless those who have injured us!

> *But to you who are listening I say: Love your enemies, do good to those who hate you, bless those who curse you, pray for those who mistreat you.* (Luke 6:28)

Here are some practical solutions to being hurt: Soak with the Lord and share the hurt or offense with Him; or share with a close trusted friend. Choose to overlook the offense or rudeness and release it when it happens. Rest in the Lord and invite Him to come and fill every cell in your body, soul, mind and spirit with his presence.

When we respond in this way we move from being self-focused, to being other focused, knowing that our needs will be met by the Lord and through those He brings to us. Respond in the Spirit, not in the flesh

Quiet yourself before the Lord right now and ask Him for three situations where you have been hurt, offended or overlooked. Now invite the Holy Spirit to come into that wounded place and wash it with His comforting presence. Forgive and release the person, group of people or church that hurt you. Invite Jesus to come in and heal you and BRING PEACE into this memory.

And finally: let's go fly a kite.

I woke up one morning to the Father saying to me. "Let's go fly your kite." I immediately had a picture in my mind of a kite having crashed behind Him in the throne room.

Then He began to talk with me about a classic movie, *Mary Poppins*[3]. In this children's musical, Mr. Banks is a very serious, severe father who never smiles. His life is dismal and his children have almost no relationship with him. Into this heavy family situation walks, well, actually flies, a governess named Mary Poppins. She immediately gets to work to transform the relationships between Mr. Banks and his children.

---

[3] Mary Poppins, Walt Disney Productions, 1964.

At the end of the movie, you see Mr. Banks released from the heaviness of his life and now enjoying the fun of flying a kite with his wife, children, boss and friends. And he is laughing, yes, actually laughing! Through the movie you never saw Mr. Banks laugh.

When the Lord said to me, "Let's go fly your kite." I had been feeling great heaviness over three parents having been hospitalized one after the other; my one brother also being hospitalized while my other brother was going blind in one eye.

All of this was extremely overwhelming for me, even though I knew the Lord would come through somehow. So when He said, "Let's go fly a kite," I realized He was talking about so much more than a kite. There is something light and fun about flying a kite, especially with family. In the midst of all my family suffering, He was telling me to enjoy Him and play with Him.

This may sound counter-intuitive to the magnitude of the situation I was facing with my family, but actually it was precisely what I needed. He wanted me to get my eyes off of the earthly sorrows and look up and join Him in play; simply enjoying His presence. That, my friends, is true faith; to release the heavy burdens and trust Father God to take care of everything.

At the end of the movie, the entire cast of *Mary Poppins* sang a song together and the Lord brought some of the verses back to me.

"When you send it flying up there all at once, you're lighter than air. You can dance on the breeze over houses and trees with your fist holding tight to the string of your kite."

The Lord wanted me to dance on the wind of His Spirit. To have a heavenly perspective in which all things are possible. Jesus flowed in miracles continually and as we embrace His perspective, allowing our minds to be renewed, we too can dance on the winds of God far above the heaviness of this world. When we choose to "fly our kites" and allow Him to transform our circumstances, then we are actually bringing down miracles from heaven.

Who of us can forget the beloved inventor and politician from the mid-1700s, Benjamin Franklin, and his famous kite connecting with lightning? The Lord reminded me of that and said that when we fly our kite with Him, we will connect with the Spirit's power, like lightning, and bring it down to earth to be released all around us.

One way to fly our kites is to remind ourselves of who He is and all the things He has done in our lives; especially healing.

I keep journals, all over my home, in which I write down answered prayers. I have done this for years now and have recorded many, many answers. Periodically I re-read all the ways He has come through and brought His kingdom into difficult situations. It is a wonderful reminder.

After being invited to fly my kite with the Lord, I now want to become more proactive in remembering not just my own answered prayers, but all the prayers He has answered for other people as well.

In conclusion, will you accept the invitation to go fly your kite with the Father, to dance on the winds of the Spirit, and believe that with God all things are possible?

Let's start a Kite Club and write down everything He has done for us and those around us. And then let's share those stories and expect His power and miracles to move through us as we fly our kite with Him.

What is impossible with man
is possible with GOD!
(Luke 18:70)

Other books by Tricia Martin

The Old Tree Series

A fantasy adventure series for the young and young at heart.

The Old Tree
The Land of Bizia
The Kingdom of Knon
The Mild, Mild West
Into the Night Sky
Arabian Lights
One for All and All for One

Tricia Martin was greatly impacted as a child by several children's fantasy books. Now years later after raising her own child, she desires to impact the hearts of children with her fantasy adventures centered around a loving, kind, and powerful character that transforms the lives of all that come into contact with Him.

She has a Masters of Arts in Counseling and belongs to the Society of Children's Book Writers and Illustrators, SCBWI.

The Old Tree; A Wonderful Edu-taining Adventure by Laurel A Basbas Ph.D. Author

"Tricia Martin's enlightening little book, "The Old Tree" is a delightful, spirited adventure with enchanting, lovable characters and a spiritually uplifting message. It is edu-tainment (education and entertainment) to be enjoyed by youngsters and by those wise enough to be young at heart. It is an invitation to color outside the lines, to see into the invisible, and to grow much larger and much smaller (as Alice in Wonderland would tell you) all in the same story. Tricia's tale entreats you to enjoy the realm of the impossibly possible! I for one, enjoyed the ride."

Sheneau Stanley-Pastor & speaker

"Tricia, uses stories to share valuable life lessons and underlying important values that kids must have to have successful lives today."

Desi d'Amani

"Enter the world of imagination, intrigue, and adventure! Whether young or younger still the Old Tree is a door into a mystical adventure where life isn't always as it appears to be and lessons are learned through overcoming. This book invites children to explore how decisions affect the world around and beyond them and it allows the childlike to re-embrace the realities of the once real but forgotten invisible realm. Step through the door into an adventure that will cause you to rethink the world as you once perceived it.

The Old Tree Series may very well be like a Chronicles of Narnia for this generation."

R. Gutierrez

The Old Tree is a portal into a kingdom where courage, hope and the promise of a new day reminds one of love's enduring presence."

Christy Peters

"Love this book. The story takes the reader on an incredible adventure. I love how Tricia was able to incorporate things from the extra-terrestrial (spirit realm) and show how they can be just as real and merged into the lives of those of us who live on the terrestrial plain. Well done and an enjoyable read for child or adult!"

Now available in paperback and e-book

The first book in The Old Tree Series

The Old Tree

Tricia Martin

Mike is bored with his summer routine. He meets a new neighbor, Mari, and together they step through an unusual tree and journey to another realm with a loving and powerful new friend. When they return home, they find a battle raging and their young lives are changed forever.

Now available in paperback and e-book

The second book in The Old Tree Series

The Land Of Bizia

Tricia Martin

Mike and Mari find themselves in a world that is on the verge of destroying itself through busyness. With the help of their loving and powerful friend, Bob, they hope to bring the people of Bizia back to the values and peace they once knew.

Now available in paperback and e-book

The third book in The Old Tree Series

The Kingdom Of Knon

Tricia Martin

Bob takes Mike and Mari to an underwater kingdom in search of an important book that has been stolen.

Now available in paperback and e-book

The fourth book in The Old Tree Series

The Mild, Mild West

Tricia Martin

Mike and Mari join an unusual creature from Bob's realm and find themselves in a western world. They need to find a way to rescue young people being stolen from their families.

Now available in paperback and e-book

The fifth book in The Old Tree Series

Into the Night Sky

Tricia Martin

Mike and Mari are joined by a British friend. They take a chariot ride into space to search for something that has been stolen from the land of Bizia.

Now available in paperback and e-book

The sixth book in The Old Tree Series

Arabian Lights

Tricia Martin

Mari's father and sister, as children, discover an unusual tree. When they walk through it they find themselves in an arid desert where a great adventure awaits them.

Now available in paperback and e-book

The seventh book in The Old Tree Series

One For All and All for One

Tricia Martin

Everything created is on the verge of destruction. Bob asks Mike and Mari to help him solve this problem.

Made in the USA
San Bernardino, CA
20 June 2017